Survival Guide:

TOP 20 Ideas How to Survive Natural Disaster in Your Home

Table of content:

Introduction: You Better Be Prepared

You have to be prepared in life, and there can be no doubt that this world gives us plenty to prep for. From brutally hot summers to ice cold winters, Mother Nature seems to be working overtime with the disasters she routinely dishes out. But if you follow the step by step instructions presented here in this book, you won't have anything to worry about. Every step of your survival is presented in perfect clarity no matter what sort of natural disaster may come your way. So, buckle up your seat belts folks, and get prepared for the ride! Because when it comes to the dangers of Mother Nature and the natural disasters she often provides, this little book is your perfect guide!

Chapter 1: Every Prepper's Nightmare—What to Avoid

You picked up this book to hear what it is you should do during a natural disaster, but just as important as knowing what to do, is knowing what *not to do*. Here in this chapter we will highlight some of the biggest mistakes, bungles, mishaps, and misnomers that people make when it comes to prepping for natural disasters. Here is what you should avoid.

Avoid Panic

The last thing that you want to do during any crisis situation is panic. If you panic you lose your focus, and if you lose your focus you could lose your life. In order to have a fixed level of concentration you need to give yourself a case of tunnel vision. Try focusing on one thing at a time, instead of scattershot distractions. Let's take for example, a sudden power outage in the middle of the night. How exactly should you handle it?

Well—instead of panicking, jumping up, bumping into the wall, and tripping and falling on your face, take a deep breath, use your cellphone as a flashlight, and make your way to the kitchen drawer where you store your candles and matches (or wherever it is that you store such things), and focus on lighting them. With this one step taken care of, you can then focus on the next. In order to avoid panic, and not be overwhelmed, strategically move from task to task until you succeed.

Don't Ignore the Authorities

In the middle of an emergency, don't be tempted to go it on your own and blatantly ignore warnings and directions from civil authorities. There are many cases of folks blatantly disregarding orders to evacuate in the face of an emergency who have failed to survive as a result. It is called the "Emergency Broadcast System" for a reason—it is meant to be broadcast as an emergency message in a time of crisis. Whatever you do, don't ignore the authorities who are in charge of your safety.

Planning at the Very Last Minute

A natural disaster should not be put off until the last minute, there are several things that you should do to prepare for the event. You should have adequate supplies at least a week ahead of time, and you should have a safehouse prepared if need be, in advance. Your home should be fortified and structurally prepped well ahead of time. Instead of planning at the last minute, make sure all of your bases are covered early on in the game.

Packing Unnecessary Things

The last thing you should do during an emergency is bog yourself down with extra baggage. If you don't need something for survival, then don't bring it. You should never waste precious time, space, and energy worrying over trivial pursuits, and instead focus on the main goal of the endeavor. All you need to pack are the necessities. Make sure you bring some food, water, and perhaps an extra pair of socks and underwear at most. Don't try to pack your whole wardrobe for an emergency evacuation from natural disaster.

Not Letting Anyone Know Where You Are

This is a major mistake that many novices make. They think they have everything under control and they don't have to tell anyone where they are or what they are doing during a disaster. But if the home you are in becomes so flooded that you have to get up on top of the roof and flag down a helicopter, it would certainly have helped if you had let others know where you were to begin with! Be sure to avoid all of these detrimental habits and behaviors as you prep for the next natural disaster.

Chapter 2: How to Survive Hurricanes, Tornadoes, and Flash Floods

From Hurricane Harvey to the tornadoes and floods that have devastated the Mid-Western United Sates, Mother Nature has dealt mankind some rather punishing blows as of late. There can be no doubt that this excessive and extreme weather has really taken its toll. But there are steps you can take to mitigate the damage and duress as much as possible. Here in this chapter we will explore your options in the face of the storm.

Have a Hurricane Evacuation Plan

The very first thing that anyone should do in the face of an oncoming hurricane is prepare an evacuation plan. You should make certain that you know the best evacuation route, and safest passage away from the danger zone. This means you should be aware of things such as elevation levels, and high-water mark regions, so that you can avoid them, and choose the quickest most secure roadways to safety. Have a go-bag to stash vital supplies in ready just in case you do have to evacuate at the last minute, and make sure that your car is full of gas. Because sometimes just being able to make a break for it is the best survival plan you could ever have.

Find a Hurricane/Tornado Safe Room

Both hurricanes and tornadoes have the potential of ripping the roof right off your house, and sending all manner of debris hurtling your way. But if you are unable to flee from an oncoming storm, you need to make sure you can go to the safest part of your home to ride it out. This usually means selecting a centralized location in the home that can then be further fortified against wind and debris. The safe room of the home is basically an improvised version of a storm shelter.

The safest place would typically be close to the middle of the structure. Bathrooms are also a fairly safe place to be, since they are typically well insulated from windows and other potentially dangerous objects. Preferably safe rooms should also be equipped with inward opening doors. This is to prevent you from getting trapped inside after the storm subsides. Because there have been many cases of folks safely riding out a storm in their safe room only to find their exit blocked by fallen debris after the storm is over.

You see, it doesn't take much for a hurricane or tornado to pin your bedroom dresser on top of your door. And if your door only opens by pushing it outward, it would be essentially blocked and locked in place by this obstruction. But if your door opens inward, rather than outward, you could still open the door and then work to push the debris out of the way. Keep all of these things in mind when prepping your hurricane and tornado safe room.

In a specific localized area, tornadoes can be just as deadly as hurricanes. And if you live in a home that is not structurally strong such as a trailer or apartment. You need to get out of them if you can. If not however, you need to hunker down and make the best of it. Just like in the above mentioned safe room, you need to find a place you can go where there are no windows, or loose and potentially hazardous debris. Once you are in this safety zone, you need to literally put your head down. If you ever did a "duck and cover" drill in school, you should know the routine.

And as the tornado hits, you need to duck down and cover your head. To further ensure your survival it wouldn't be a bad idea to get under a strong table or desk, this structure could serve as a barrier and shield to protect you from falling and flying debris.

And if you happen to be out on the road when the storm hits, you need to find shelter immediately. Do not try to outrace the storm, because unlike what you may have seen in the movies, cars are just not equipped to drive that fast!

On average, tornadoes travel at speeds in excess of 100 miles an hour! And even if you think your souped-up hotrod can go from zero to 120 miles an hour, it doesn't matter.

Because you have to realize, that unlike you, the tornado doesn't have to travel along the roadways, it is free to go in any and every direction. And while you are sitting in your car watching a twister right in front of you, it could change course and head your way in an instant.

By the time you struggle to put your car in reverse to turn around, it will be too late. If you want to survive a tornado, you are going to want to stay off the roads. And if you do find yourself driving when a tornado hits, and unable to get to shelter immediately, the best thing for you to do is to get out of the car and head for a ditch. Getting down low to the ground inside a ditch is probably the best protection you could find in such a situation, so don't hesitate to do it.

Surviving Flash Floods

Finding yourself suddenly at the mercy of a flash flood is no easy thing to deal with. They are called "flash" floods for a reason, because these guys are as fast as a flash! Just picture it. You are driving down the road in a rain storm and the next thing you know you have water up to your driver's side window. That is just how rapidly things can deteriorate when you are dealing with flash floods. If you are inside your vehicle and find yourself subjected to a natural disaster like this, you need to immediately turn around and drive for higher ground.

And if you are unable to drive to safety—then by all means—get out of the car and make a run for it on foot! Remember, your life is more important than your car! You can always get another vehicle but you can't get another life! Be advised that in some circumstances with rapidly rising water you may not be able to get your door open in time. This is due to water pressure on the door. If you find this to be the case, the best thing to do is just bust open your window. An easy way to do this, is to grab hole of your metal seat belt buckle and smash it right into the glass.

At any rate, you need to break the window, and climb out as soon as possible. If you are walking out on foot and notice that the water level is rising, stay away from any naturally occurring bodies of water. If you are near a river, move away from the river edge, near a lake walk in the other direction, and so on and so forth. Also, if you are in a wilderness environment and happen to notice high water marks on trees and other landmarks—even if it is not flooded at the moment—this is a clear indication that this is an area that is particularly vulnerable to flash floods, and should be avoided if heavy rain begins to descend. This is how you can survive a flash flood.

Chapter 3: How to Survive the Worst of the Winter

Recent winter weather has been particularly harsh. And even while the debate rages on over climate change and global warming, many of us in the Northern Hemisphere find ourselves routinely snowed in from December to February. We often hear phrases and terms such as "arctic blast" and "polar vortexes". But all we really know as that bone cold air hits us right in the face, as we shovel and scrape our way out of the blizzard, is that the extremes of winter weather have just made our lives that much more difficult. This chapter provides you with the tip and tricks you need to dig yourself out of the worst of the winter.

Pack Some Warm Clothes

The last thing you want to do during horribly cold winter weather is go out underdressed or without warm clothing. The key to staying warm during the winter months is to wear layers. You should always wear an undershirt, an over shirt, a light sweater, coat, overcoat, and a warm pair of gloves. These layers will help shield you from the winter frost. You should also cover your head. They say that about half of all our body heat escapes right out of our heads every single day. So, cover your head with a warm winter hat to stay warm.

Prep a Fire Drill

Yes, my friends, this is indeed still a book on winter prep, and no, we are not speaking of the weekly "Fire Drills" you had in Middle School in which you had to line up and pretend your school was on fire. Nope, that is not what we are talking about here. The "fire drill" we speak of in this section is actually an ancient fire-starting tool of the Native Americans, in which a stick or finely carved piece of wood is rolled between the hands and "drilled" into a board of wood to spark a campfire.

Anyone who finds themselves stuck out in the cold tundra could make use of this simple but effective device. Now, for the sake of clarity, let me repeat one more time how this contraption is used. Basically, you just take a stick, approximately a foot or two long, and you stand it up on a thin wooden board. This board is actually referred to as a "fire board" but its essentially just a thin piece of wood. Situate your fire drill upright on the fireboard, and place the upper mid-section of the stick between your two outstretched, flat palms.

Vigorously roll the fire drill back and forth with the bottom of the stick quickly spinning against the surface of the fireboard. This action is what creates the friction that will spark a fire. Use this spark to set any tinder you have, such as twigs, leaves, charcoal, or whatever else you have, ablaze. Knowing how to prep a fire drill is a great skill to have, and a guaranteed way to stay warm in the cold.

Get a Blizzard Bag

If you get hit with the blizzard bug, then you should get yourself a blizzard bag. This means gathering together a bag of emergency supplies that you would use during a bad snow storm. In this blizzard bag you should have, a good snow shovel, ice scrapers, and any other tool that might be important when it comes to digging through wet and snowy weather. Along with these, you should also make sure to stash a conventional flashlight, batteries, a cell phone charger, and even a bag of cat litter. Yes—cat litter! Many people are not aware of it, but cat litter works wonders when it comes to cars stuck in the snow. Just put a little bit of cat litter underneath your stuck tires, give it a little gas and you are good to go!

Use Sun Absorbent Windows

Even under the best of circumstances, winter weather can get rather chilly, rather fast. But imagine just how bad things would get if your power were to go out, and you have no other means of heating. Your home and your body temperature would get dangerously cold in a relatively short period of time.

But even with no other recourse, all you have to do is look to that yellow ball of gas in the sky, and the sun to bail you out! Even in the coldest of winters, the sun still manages to shine down on us for at least a few hours every day.

If you could just capture some of those rays and use them for your advantage you could spare yourself much of the cold. The best way to do this is to turn your homes windows into mini solar sun absorbers. This is done by taking a piece of cardboard and cutting it into the shape of your windows. Now take some black spray paint and thoroughly coat the board with black paint. Black, is of course a sun absorbent material. Put this black cardboard up into your windows to absorb sunlight. These simple, yet incredibly useful, solar attracting boards, will now heat up your home in no time.

Apply Insulation and Weather Stripping

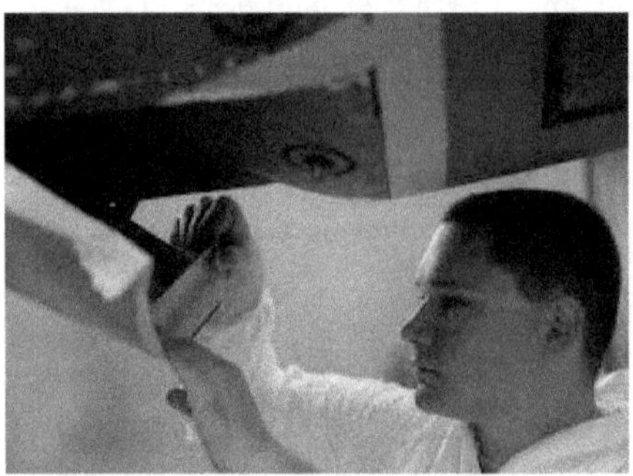

It can't be stressed enough how important good insulation and weather stripping really are. Most homes lose a lot of heat through cracks in their doors and windows, but if you were to just put some thin layers of weather stripping inside to fill those gaps, the heat of the home will be retained. The easiest way to pinpoint these gaps in doors and windows is to hold a lit flame, such as a match or cigarette lighter up to the frames of your doors and watch as drafts move the flame, these drafts will indicate the exact spots you need to install your weather stripping.

As for the insulation of your home, you should take care to make sure that draft prone areas such as your attic are adequately insulated. In order to avoid gusts of cold wind blowing into your home and warm air seeping out, make sure you put sufficient layers of insulation up in the rafters of the attic. As it turns out, your attic is the structural head of your house, and about half all your homes heat seeps out of it. So just like you need to put a warm hat on your own head during the winter months, you should put a warm hat on the roof of your home by insulating your attic.

Can and Store Plenty of Food, Store Excess Water

Canning has kept populations all over the globe well fed in even the worst of circumstances. And it is completely feasible for someone to store up as much as a year's worth of food through the process of simply canning them in pressurized jars. Canning can preserve the integrity of food almost indefinitely. All you have to do to can your own jars is find a typical "mason jar" and stuff it with your produce. Next, put a sealing lid on the jar, tighten it, and place the jar in the center of a pot full of boiling hot water. Allow it to boil and pressurize for several minutes, and your food for the winter is canned!

Even more important than food is having an adequate supply of drinkable water. Because believe me—in the middle of a winter storm you don't want to have to resort to drinking that funny looking yellow snow you found outside! So, in order to avoid this fate, be sure to pack several bottles of water before the snowy weather hits. In an emergency you can also tap into excess water from your water heater, and even water in your toilet tank! Hey—it may not always be pretty—but it's survival!

Chapter 4: Surviving Fire and Earthquakes

If you live on the West Coast of the United States, the two biggest threats that you face are out of control wild fires and unpredictable Earth tremors, all the way to devastating earthquakes. In this chapter we highlight some of the best ways to handle and manage these life-impacting natural disasters.

Fire Preparedness

The first step in ensuring your survival is always preparation. And this couldn't be truer than when it comes to fire safety. You need to have your smoke detectors checked frequently and you need to have a clear path to exit your home. The number one problem that many face when confronted with a fire is not having an adequate way out the door. Make sure that the hallway is clear of clutter and your doors free of debris, so that you can point yourself, and your loved ones in the right direction. As you can see, just being prepared is half the battle.

Surviving the Blaze

If you find yourself caught right in the middle of a fire, the first thing you need to do is get down as low to the ground as possible. The reason for this is quite simple. Heat rises. This means then, that during the course of a fire, the upper levels of the home will be much hotter than the lower levels. The level of heat could fluctuate to such an extent, that the ceiling of a home on fire, could be as hot as a roasting oven, while the floor remains just a few degrees above normal room temperature.

Also, the smoke of the fire will no doubt be the most prolific up in the rafters then down on the ground. So, get down on the floor and crawl to the exit. And if you can't get to an immediate exit door, you might have to make one. If you are near a picture window for example, you could take an object or even your bear hands to break it open. If you do get to a door however, before reaching for that doorknob, it would be wise to remember that this door knob may very well be red hot.

If it is, you can take off your shirt, or some other article of clothing and use it as a kind of protective glove—if you will—and with its protection from the heat, you can quickly fling the door open, and make your escape. As soon as you are out, position yourself far away from the flames as you wait for first responders to arrive. If you keep all of these tips and precautions in mind, you will be able to survive the blaze completely unscathed.

Healing Burns with Aloe Vera

If you have ever been burned you know just how horrible it feels. Our skin is our point of contact with the outside world, and when it is significantly damaged through a bad burn, even a sudden breeze against its surface could be excruciating. And as much as we can try to prepare for the calamity that a fire would represent, there is always the chance we could be caught off guard enough to suffer a burn injury.

If this is the case, you need to take immediate measures to make sure that the injury does not get worse. This means that you need to bandage the injured part of your body up and place ointment on its surface. One of the best ointments for this task is Aloe Vera. Aloe Vera gel scooped directly out of the Aloe Vera plant is soothing and healing. Just place it right on the skin and wrap the injured area up, and you will be on the road to recovery in no time.

Predicting the Big Quake

The vast majority of us, are probably under the assumption that earthquakes are a far away problem, that would never affect us. If you live in North America for example, you no doubt associate a quake with the West Coast. But despite what you may think, there are many more places other than California and Oregon that are subjected to quakes. The truth is, an earthquake can happen anywhere. The only reason that we are led to believe that earthquakes only happen in certain locations is because of how earthquakes are forecast.

You see, while there is no doppler radar that can spot big quakes, several days ahead of time, quakes are predicted by statistics and past precedent. But in the end, this form of statistical reasoning is not an exact science, and merely a hypothetical guess at best. In reality, earthquakes can occur anywhere, at any time. In fact, the biggest earthquake on record is not on the West Coast at all—it occurred right in the middle of the nation in Missouri. Yes, Missouri.

In 1811 an earthquake hit the state of Missouri that was said to be so powerful, that it caused rooftop chimneys to collapse as far away as Cincinnati, Ohio! So, having that said, we cannot always rely on statistical averages when it comes to predicting the next big quake. The truth of the matter is, an earthquake can happen anytime, anywhere, so no matter where we are located, we must be prepared.

Dealing with the Aftermath of an Earthquake

During an earthquake there are several things that you should consider. You should make sure that you have a safe place to ride out the quake away from falling debris, this is rather obvious. But what people often forget is how to deal with the aftermath. In order to prevent hazardous conditions in your home after a quake, you need to turn off the electric, water and gas utilities.

Because in the aftermath of a quake, all of these could pose a potential hazard. Ruptured pipes can flood the home, gas lines could burst and create an explosive hazard, and ripped electrical lines can lead to electrocution. In the aftermath of the quake, make sure that all of these things are taken care of, and accounted for.

Conclusion: Home Grown Survival

The world is full of danger, and crisis can strike us at a moment's notice. But even though natural disasters are on the rise, that doesn't mean that we can't prepare for it. And if you take the 20 proven survival strategies presented in this book to heart, regardless of the occasion or the natural disaster—wind, rain, sleet, earthquake, or snow—you will be able to make it through. Because home is where the heart is, and when it comes to natural disasters and all the other threats we face, a little home-grown survival could do us all a whole lot of good.